<u>forgotten</u>

A selection of photographs of Newcastle upon Tyne in the 1960's.

Newcastle City Libraries

Introduction to Third Edition

When we first published this booklet in the Summer of 1984, we little realised quite the impact it would make on the Newcastle public. Even a second edition failed to satiate demand and has led us to publish this, the third edition.

Our awareness of the strong desire for local nostalgia, ably demonstrated by the success of the first booklet, quickly led to the production of 'Gone... but not forgotten 2' (a local bestseller!) and, most recently, 'Gone... but not forgotten 3; Trams, Trains, Trolleys'. Whereas the content of this booklet remains as originally envisaged we have taken the opportunity of redesigning the front cover to bring it in line with its 'stable-mates'.

Introduction to First and Second Edition

Councillor F.H. Bell, who died in 1966, was a man of vision and humanity. He was impressed by the York City Guide Service and the significant part it played in explaining and publicizing that historic city. He persuaded the Newcastle City Council to establish a similar body of voluntary trained guides, to be operated by the City Library.

The Newcastle University Department of Adult Education began, in 1962, the initial training of the volunteers, to ensure that their subject knowledge was sound and that they could communicate that knowledge. This was to form the basis of subsequent training. In 1963 the first conducted tours took place, and in the following year the service was formally constituted at a Mansion House reception when the Lord Mayor presented nineteen guides with their badges. Although based on the Central Library the guides are a self-regulating body with their own committee, and it is this committee which trains and retrains guides and keeps the service responsive to city changes.

We are celebrating 21 years of a voluntary service in which the city can take great pride. Indeed the popularity has exceeded the expectations of its founders: 1,600 persons in the first year have increased to an average of 4,000, including parties from outside the city and from foreign countries. In addition to conducting tours and giving talks some guides have, through their own work, added to our knowledge of the city's history, especially of the suburbs, areas which tend to fall outside the scope of the standard local histories.

The past 21 years have seen considerable change, caused by the city redevelopment plan; the photographs here reflect some of the changes. When tours began in 1963 the Quayside chares were still intact. The old town hall still stood, and the Victorian central library with its richly carved facade. But with work already begun on the Pilgrim Street roundabout the demolition of Dobson's Royal Arcade was imminent The Empire Theatre, Newgate Street, was closed in 1963 for eventual demolition. (The thistle on its facade commemorated the ancient Scotch Inn on the same site where visiting Scottish Kings had lodged). Cooks corner, Northumberland Street, a famous point of reference, has gone, and the Olympia cinema,

Northumberland Road, formerly a music hall. The construction of the Eldon Square shopping centre caused the disappearance of more famous buildings: Dobson's greenmarket and two sides of his Eldon Square; the fishmarket; "Bourgognes", an old inn built in 1634; and Prudhoe Street.

The fine covered Grainger Market remains, and happily Blackfriars, Holy Jesus Hospital and Keelman's Hospital, three of the city's oldest buildings have been excellently restored and put to use. The Plummer and Sallyport towers, and the Guildhall were restored soon after tours began. This period saw the appearance of some of the city's finest new buildings, particularly the Civic Centre and University developments.

The increasing importance which the local authorities attach to tourism is evidenced by the care taken in preserving and enhancing the Grainger-Dobson area; by the landscaping of historic buildings; and by the Tyne and Wear County Council historic plaques. These policies encourage the enthusiasts in the now well-established city guide service to continue their fascinating and strenuous work of publicizing this historic and proud city of Newcastle upon Tyne.

ARTHUR WALLACE
Vice-President, Association of City Guides
of Newcastle upon Tyne.

June, 1984

1. The Bigg Market and the old Town Hall in 1966. The Town Hall
   was then used for shows and exhibitions: it was demolished in
   1970.

2. The Empire Theatre, Newgate Street shortly after closure in 1963. Originally opened as a Music Hall in 1890, it was extensively rebuilt in 1902-03. Although officially the 'Empire Palace', it was always known simply as 'The Empire'. The Newgate Shopping Centre occupies its site.

3. Newgate Street, opposite St. Andrew's Church looking North. From the Middle Ages many of the town's markets were held in this area, an activity carried on until the buildings were demolished for the Eldon Square Shopping Precinct. Photographed in 1964.

4. The Green Market (or Fruit and Vegetable Market) just before it closed in 1970. The new Green Market is on the same site. The wholesale traders from the old Green Market moved to the Team Valley Trading Estate.

5. The Fish Market on the corner of Clayton Street and St. Andrew's Street in 1965. It opened here in the nineteenth century and for many years had an upper storey in which live birds and pets were sold. The new Fish Market stands on the same site.

6. Newgate Street, looking north towards Percy Street in about 1966. Almost all the buildings on the right are pubs - 'The Bacchus', 'Bourgognes' and on the corner of Blackett Street, the 'King's Head'. All were demolished for Eldon Square.

7. 'The Bacchus' on the corner of Newgate Street and High Friar Street in 1964. This Victorian Inn was built on the site of a much older building of the same name.

8. One of Newcastle's oldest pubs dating from the seventeenth century, 'Bourgognes' was originally known as the Mason's Arms and took its more familiar name from the family who were its landlords from the late nineteenth century. Photographed in 1964.

9. Prudhoe Street, looking from Percy Street towards Northumberland Street in 1966. Halfway down on the left was the Prudhoe Street Mission, popularly known as 'Daddy Bowran's Mission'. It moved to the top of Westgate Hill when the area was redeveloped.

10. The Haymarket Bus Station in 1966. Hay was sold here from 1824 until early in the present century. The 'Tatler Cartoon Cinema' became the 'Classic', then a private members cinema and is now closed. The Bus Station has been redesigned and rebuilt.

11. A view of the Haymarket in 1960, showing the South African War Memorial and one of the Newcastle's trolleybuses. The Haymarket Metro Station now occupies much of the foreground.

12. St. Thomas's Church, the Haymarket and the top of Northumberland Street in 1964.

13. Northumberland Road looking east from Northumberland
Street. British Home Stores opened in 1932, and was completely
rebuilt in the early 1970's. The other building is the former
Olympia Cinema closed in 1961. Photographed in 1966.

14. The 'Northumberland Arms', corner of Northumberland Street and Prudhoe Street in 1970. It was latterly the only pub in Northumberland Street and a new 'Northumberland Arms' was built on roughly the same site at the entrance to Eldon Square.

15.   The foot of Northumberland Street in 1966. The decorative
plaster work on Amos Atkinson's shop was completed in 1953 to
celebrate the Coronation.

16. The junction of Northumberland Street and New Bridge Street, popularly known as "Cook's Corner". The footbridge was one of two erected in Northumberland Street in 1967. The Pearl Assurance Buildings were erected early in the century.

17. Blackett Street looking west in 1955. The Y.M.C.A. was built in 1900, but the buildings beyond date from the 1820's. All the buildings on the left of the street were demolished for Eldon Square.

18.　Blackett Street below a network of trolley wires. Trolleybuses ran in Newcastle from 1935 and were withdrawn in 1966 at about the time this picture was taken.

19. A view of old Eldon Square from Grey's Monument. The dome in the foreground is of the Y.M.C.A. The north and west sides of the square, seen here, have been demolished. Photographed in 1967.